ANIMAL CHAMPIONS

by Teri Crawford Jones

Modern Curriculum Press

An Imprint of Pearson Learning
299 Jefferson Road, P.O. Box 480
Parsippany, NJ 07054 - 0480

Internet address:
http://www.mcschool.com

Credits

Illustrations: 20–21, 29, 34, 38t.: Patrick Gnan/Deborah Wolfe Ltd.

Photos: Front cover: Tim Davis/Tony Stone Images. Title page: Fritz Polking/Dembinsky Photo Associates. 5: Superstock. 6: Ken Redmond Photography. 7: Alexander Zemlianichenko/AP/Wide World Photos. 8: Lori Adamski Peck/Tony Stone Images. 9: Superstock. 10: Fritz Polking/Dembinsky Photo Associates. 11: Rod Planck/Tom Stack & Associates. 12: t. Leonard Lee Rue III; b. Fernandez & Peck/Adventure Photo & Film. 13: C.D. Giussolli/FPG International. 14: Superstock. 15: © C.K. Loreny/The National Audubon Society Collection/Photo Researchers, Inc. 16: © Leonard Lee Rue/The National Audubon Society Collection/Photo Researchers, Inc. 17: t. Gary Milburn/Tom Stack & Associates; b. © Fletcher & Bayliss/The National Audubon Society Collection/Photo Researchers, Inc. 18. b.l. Randy Wells/Tony Stone Images; b.r. Bob Gomel/The Stock Market. 19: b.l. © Renee Lynn/The National Audubon Society Collection/Photo Researchers, Inc.; b.r. Tim Davis/The National Audubon Society Collection/Photo Researchers, Inc. 22: Norbert Wu/Tony Stone Images. 23: R.E. Barber Nature Photography. 24: t. Alan G. Nelson/Dembinsky Photo Associates; b. Randa Bishop/Uniphoto Picture Agency. 25: David W. Hamilton/The Image Bank. 26: Laurie Campbell/Tony Stone Images. 27: Leonard Lee Rue III/Visuals Unlimited. 28: Leonard Rue, Jr. 30: Gerard Lacy/Peter Arnold, Inc. 31: t. Larry Tackett/Tom Stack & Associates; b. PhotoDisc, Inc. 32: Chris Johns/Tony Stone Images. 33: © Fred Tilly/Photo Researchers, Inc. 35: Desmond Burdon/Tony Stone Images. 36. David Sutton/Uniphoto Picture Agency. 37: Randy Napier/Uniphoto Picture Agency. 38: b. Stan Osolinski/Dembinsky Photo Associates. 39: R.E. Barber Nature Photography. 40: t. Carl Cook Photography; b. W. Perry Conway/Uniphoto Picture Agency. 41: t., b. Peter Drowne/Color-Pic, Inc. 42: © Gijsbert van Frankenhuyzen/Dembinsky Photo Associates. 43: © Jeff Lepore/Photo Researchers, Inc. 44: Jay Alex Langley/Uniphoto Picture Agency. 45: © Bud Lehnhausen/Photo Researchers, Inc. 46: t. Gary Schultz; b. Gary Meszaros/Dembinsky Photo Associates. 47. Fernandez & Peck/Adventure Photo & Film.

Design by Agatha Jaspon and Dorothea Fox

ISBN: 0–7652–0877–6

3 4 5 6 7 8 9 10 SP 05 04 03 02 01 00 99

CONTENTS

Let the Games Begin!

People around the world love sports. They like to run, jump, throw balls, skate, ski, and swim. They also like to watch sports. The biggest sports event of all is held every two years. This event is called the Olympic games.

Olympic torch

The Olympics take place in the summer or in the winter. In the summer the athletes swim and dive in a pool. They run and jump on a track. They play basketball, too.

Olympic diver

Olympic freestyle skier

In the winter they ski down a snow-covered hill. They skate on ice. They sled down an icy track.

The best athletes from around the world come to the Olympics. In some sports, judges watch and score what the athletes can do. Then they choose the champions.

Olympic hurdler

Champion athletes can do many things. However, they aren't the only champions in the world. Have you ever thought about what animals can do? Many animals can swim, run, and dive better than humans do. Let's take a look at some animal athletes around the world.

On Your Mark, Get Set, Go!

Animals run for many reasons. Some run to catch food. Others run away from animals that want to eat them. Young animals may run just for fun. What animals do you think are the fastest runners?

Horse running

Cheetah

The cheetah is the fastest runner for a short distance. This spotted cat covers the ground at a top speed of 70 miles an hour across the African grasslands. This is faster than many speed limits for cars.

How can the cheetah run so fast? Look at its lean body and long legs. A cheetah's backbone also bends easily. The cheetah can bend and stretch with each step.

The pronghorn antelope is almost as fast as the cheetah. It runs up to 60 miles an hour. The pronghorn lives in herds in grasslands in the American Southwest. It gets its name from the shape of its horns, which look like prongs, or the pointed ends of a fork. Both males and females have these horns.

Pronghorn antelope

Wildebeest

Lion

The wildebeest and the lion are also champion runners that live in Africa. They both can run about 50 miles an hour.

A baby wildebeest is ready to run 30 minutes after it is born. It has to be able to get away from the lions that hunt wildebeests for food.

Of course these animals do not race against each other like people do. If they did, which animal do you think would win? Look again at how fast each animal can run.

Amazing Facts

- ► A human's top speed is just under 28 miles an hour. A human could outrun an elephant, which runs about 25 miles an hour.

- ► Other animals that are slower than humans include the wild turkey, the pig, and the chicken.

- ► The slowest animal of all is the garden snail. It would take a snail almost half an hour just to cross a sidewalk.

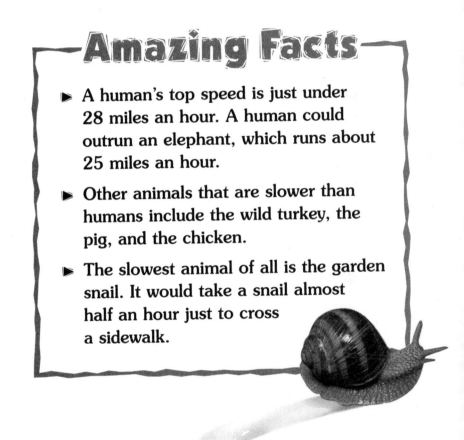

CHAPTER 3

All the Way to the Top

People need special equipment such as ropes to climb mountains. Many animals are champion climbers without any help.

Feet are the secret to mountain climbing. The Rocky Mountain goat can leap from rock to rock and never slip. Each hoof, or foot, is split. It has a hard outside and a soft inside so it can bend over rocks and hold onto them.

Rocky Mountain
goat

The African klipspringer (or "cliff springer") also has unusual feet. It stands on its toenails. This deer-like animal has hooves like no other animal's. The toenails grow down. They look like pegs.

When the klipspringer jumps, it can land on a spot no bigger than a silver dollar. A spot that size is less than two inches across.

Klipspringer

Squirrel

Some animals climb trees instead of mountains. The squirrel can race down a branch and leap to another branch without even stopping. It can hang upside down on a tree trunk. The secret is its sharp claws. They dig into the bark and keep the squirrel from falling.

The tree hyrax is another champion climber. This little animal lives in Africa and spends most of its time in trees. The little suction cups on its feet help it hold onto the tree bark.

Tree hyrax

The squirrel is a faster climber than the hyrax. Sometimes the squirrel falls though. The hyrax never falls. If these animals were in a climbing race, which one do you think would win the prize?

Amazing Facts

Have you ever heard of a fish climbing a tree? The mudskipper can live both on land and in water. On land, it will climb on fallen trees and rocks. It uses its fins to hang onto the tree bark or the rocks.

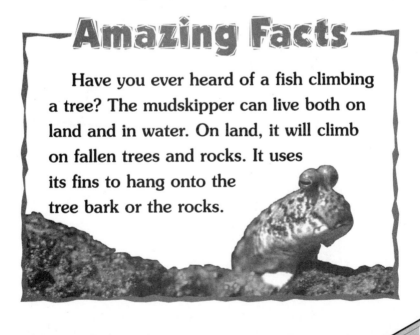

Fast Swimmers and Deep Divers!

Besides running and climbing, animals also swim and dive just like people do. What animals do you think are champion swimmers and divers?

The sailfish can swim up to 68 miles an hour. That is faster than most boats. You can see sailfish in the Atlantic Ocean, near Florida. The marlin also lives in the Atlantic. It can swim up to 50 miles an hour.

Marlin

Sailfish

The dolphin can swim at just over 18 miles an hour. It has slick, rubbery skin that slides easily through water. Even though it lives in the ocean, the dolphin is not a fish. It is a mammal. It has to come up to the top of the water to breathe air.

The penguin is a fast-swimming seabird that spends a lot of time in the ocean. Its thick layer of feathers are waterproof. The penguin uses its strong wings, which look like flippers, to push itself through the water.

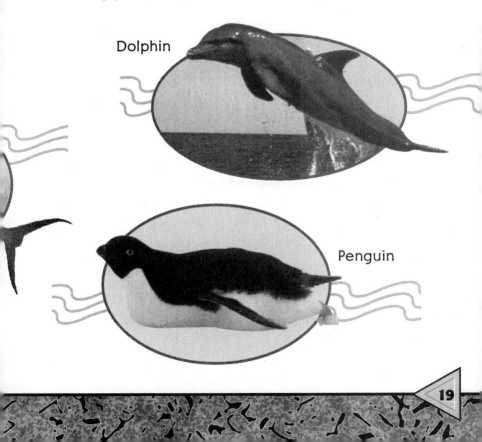

Dolphin

Penguin

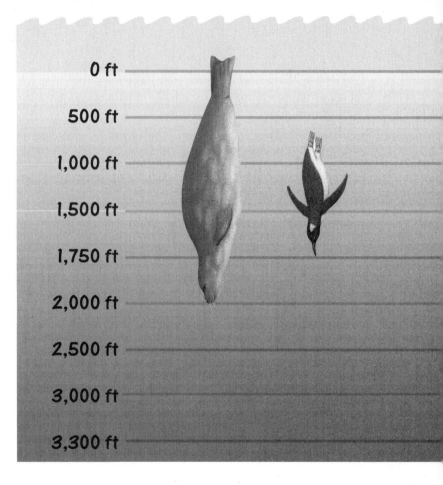

0 ft	
500 ft	
1,000 ft	
1,500 ft	
1,750 ft	
2,000 ft	
2,500 ft	
3,000 ft	
3,300 ft	

How deep can ocean animals dive? Let's watch the penguin first. It can dive down to 1,750 feet before coming back up for air. In the cold sea, the penguin dives deep to find fish to eat.

The Weddell seal swims under the ice in Antarctica. It can dive as deep as 2,000 feet in just five minutes.

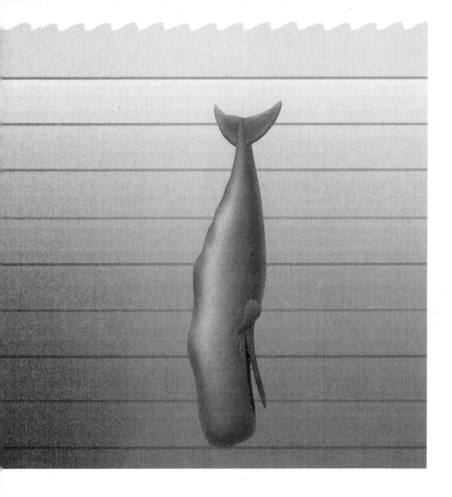

The whale makes the deepest dive. It goes down 3,300 feet. The whale can stay under water for over an hour before coming back up for air. The whale dives to find food. A whale may go even deeper than 3,300 feet if it is chasing a tasty dinner.

Sea animals dive to find food. Look back at the graph on pages 20-21. If these animals were in a contest, who do you think would win? Look at the numbers. Which animal dived deepest?

Amazing Facts

▶ Below the lowest point of the whale's dive, the ocean is dark. There is no light that far down. Fish that live in the deepest part of the ocean cannot see. They use other senses, like touch, to find their way.

▶ The angler fish lives on the ocean bottom. It hunts for food with its own light. On the end of a thin growth from its head is a flap of skin. A chemical in the skin makes it glow. Fish are drawn to the light. Then the angler fish has a tasty dinner.

Champions Fly High

Many animals can do something that people can only do with gliders or airplanes. They can fly!

One of the sky champions is the frigate bird. This speedy bird can fly up to 95 miles an hour. It skims along the top of the ocean looking for food.

Frigate bird

Another fast-flying bird is the mallard duck. It can fly up to 65 miles an hour. Mallards live all over the United States and in Canada. A male mallard is easily seen. It has a shiny green head.

Mallard

Albatross

Some birds are sky champions because they fly long distances. Instead of flapping its wings, the albatross glides over the ocean. It has long, narrow wings that catch the air currents. The albatross may travel up to 9,000 miles looking for food.

The Arctic tern travels from the North
Pole to the South Pole. It may fly more than
11,000 miles. The record flight set so far is
14,000 miles in 10 months.

Arctic tern

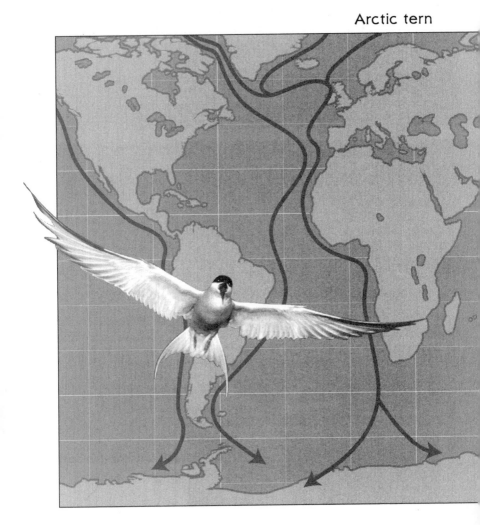

A few animals can fly without wings. They are the Alaskan flying squirrel, the butterfly lizard, and the East Indian paradise tree snake. All of them either use flaps of skin or flatten their bodies to fly. Then they make themselves like little parachutes. They ride the air and glide down to the ground.

Animal Gymnastics

Have you ever watched human gymnasts tumble and swing? The best human gymnasts could never do the moves some animals can do.

Hummingbird's wings in motion

The hummingbird is a champion gymnast. It flies like a little helicopter. A hummingbird can hover in midair. It can turn upside down or fly backward. Sometimes it flies straight up and then forward. Its wings move so fast that you see only a blur.

Part of this bird's secret is how it moves its wings. Its wings don't flap up and down. They move forward and backward. The hummingbird also has very strong wing muscles.

The cat is also a champion gymnast. Have you heard that a cat will always land on its feet? This is only true if the cat falls more than 100 feet.

When it falls, the cat flips right side up. It spreads its legs and flattens its body. By doing this, the cat traps air with its body. This helps to slow the fall. When it lands, the cat bends its legs to soften the shock.

How a cat falls

The monkey is another great gymnast. It has long fingers and arms. Its long tail can wrap around branches. The monkey uses its hands and tail to leap and swing from tree to tree.

Squirrel monkey

Amazing Facts

Have you ever seen a gymnast swing on a rope? A spider carries its own rope. It uses a special liquid in its body to spin a silk thread. It attaches the thread to a leaf. If the spider jumps from a branch, the thread keeps it from falling to the ground.

CHAPTER 7

Watch and Listen!

Animals also can do quiet things well. Their eyes and ears can hear sounds and see things that people would never notice.

Eyes and ears help animals find food. They watch and listen for danger, too. How do you think human sight and hearing compare to that of animals?

Jack rabbit

Hawk

If animals could read, from how far away would they be able to read the words in a book? Suppose that you put an open book on the ground. You might be able to read the book from 5 feet away. A dog could read it from 10 feet away.

The hawk is the real champion. It could read the book from 230 feet away. The hawk needs sharp eyes because it is a bird of prey. This means it eats other animals, such as mice. From far up in the sky, the hawk can spot a mouse on the ground.

The owl has sharp eyes, too. Its eyes are sharp in a special way. As a bird of prey, the owl hunts only at night. It can see shapes and outlines. However, it can't see colors. Have you ever tried to see something in a dark room? The owl can see everything you can't.

Owl's view

Human's view

Cat's reflecting eyes

The cat can't see as far as the hawk or as well as the owl. Yet at night it too can see very well. Its special eyes reflect light twice. Your eyes reflect light only once. Also, the cat's eyes are set in the front of its head. This gives the cat 3-D sight. You have 3-D sight, too. This means you can see an object's height, length, and width.

Sounds are like waves in the air. Small, fast waves are heard by our ears as high sounds. Big, slow waves are heard as low sounds.

Smaller animals can hear higher sounds. Bigger animals can hear lower sounds. People cannot hear as well as many animals, but they are better at knowing where sounds come from.

Dogs can hear higher sounds than people can hear. If you blow a dog whistle, you won't hear anything. A dog hears the whistle loud and clear.

Dog

Owl

The owl uses its ears to find food. It can hear a little mouse move. Its ears tell it where to find the mouse.

Why does the owl hear so well? It has one ear placed higher than the other. One ear also points down while the other one points up. This makes it easy for the owl to hear small sounds.

Owls can also remember from where they heard a sound. Then, a few minutes later, they can fly down to the ground to catch a mouse.

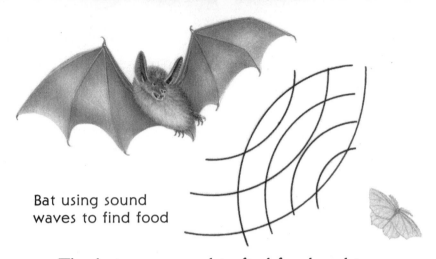

Bat using sound
waves to find food

The bat uses sound to find food and to know where it is going. It makes sounds that bounce off things. When the sounds come back to the bat's ears, it knows there is something ahead. There might be a bug to eat. There might also be something the bat needs to fly around.

Amazing Facts

Ears are good for other things besides hearing. The fennec fox lives in the desert. Its ears are huge. These big ears help the fox stay cool. They also help get rid of body heat.

A Good Defense

In the Olympic sports of boxing and fencing, athletes use boxing gloves or swords to defend themselves. Animals can defend themselves with their teeth, hooves, or claws. They also climb trees or run away from danger. What about animals who can't do these things? What do they do?

The skunk is well known for its defense. It just lifts its tail and sprays its enemy with a terrible-smelling liquid. The liquid comes from glands at the base of its tail.

Baby skunks

Most of the porcupine's body is covered with up to 30,000 sharp needles, or quills. When it is scared or angry, the porcupine curls up and tightens its skin. If anything touches the quills, they come out. The quills stick and stab whatever is bothering the porcupine.

Porcupine needle

Porcupine

Armadillo

The armadillo from South America and the southern United States has a hard outer covering like armor. When in danger, it curls tightly into a ball. Then it rolls away.

Opossum

The North American opossum can't run fast from danger. So it suddenly drops dead. At least it looks dead. It pretends so well that other animals think the opossum is dead. So they leave it alone. Some people think the opossum just faints because it is so scared.

Many other animals have interesting defenses. Turtles have shells. Lizards have tails that break off if another animal bites them. Which defense do you think is the most amazing?

Amazing Facts

Some animals pretend to be hurt to save others. A bird called the killdeer acts as if it has a broken wing. An animal thinks the mother bird will be easy to catch. It follows the killdeer away from the bird's nest. Then the killdeer just flies away.

To All a Good Night

One thing many animals and people do very well is sleep. Everyone needs to sleep. Sleep helps animals have energy to find food and to play.

The koala sleeps about 22 hours a day. This means it has only 2 hours each day to eat and move around its tree home in Australia. The sloth is a close second. It sleeps 20 hours. The armadillo snoozes for 19 hours a day.

Koala

Sloth

Some animals sleep for months. This special kind of sleep is called hibernation. Animals hibernate because they live where winter is very cold. There is also little food when it is cold. So the animals find a safe place. Then they sleep for weeks or months until it is warmer outside. A hibernating animal's heart slows down. The animal breathes very slowly. It hardly moves at all.

The Barrow ground squirrel hibernates for 9 months every year. A chipmunk also hibernates for many weeks.

Polar bear

You may have heard that bears hibernate. However, a bear just sleeps for most of the winter. Every few weeks it wakes up. It may go outside its den and look around for something to eat.

Amazing Facts

Some animals barely sleep at all. The shrew, for example, uses a lot of energy. So it has to eat its weight in food every three hours. It has almost no time to sleep.

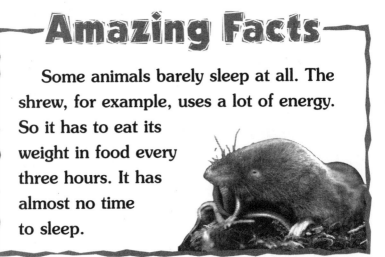

As you can see, animals can do many different things. Some things they can do better than people can. If animals were in the Olympics, which events do you think they would be in? How do you think they would do?

Lion

GLOSSARY

athletes (ATH leets) people trained in sports and exercises of strength, speed, and skill

champions (CHAM pee uns) people, animals, or things that are the best in a game or contest

contest (KAHN test) something that tests a skill or ability, such as a race or a game

defense (dee FENS) an act protecting oneself against attack or injury

gymnastics (jihm NAS tihks) exercises in which athletes tumble, swing, and balance on beams

hibernate (HYE bur nayt) to be inactive over a long period of time; some animals hibernate in winter

judges (JUJ ihz) people who watch a contest and decide who the winner is

reflect (rih FLEKT) to throw back something, such as light, heat, or sound

sports (sports) games or contests that are usually physical and involve some competition

suction (SUK shun) an act of drawing air out of space to make something stick to a surface